POLICE BRUTALITY + CRIME + WELFARE = BIRTH CONTROL

Carolyn Franklin M.A.

Carolyn Franklin M.A.

voicedynamicscf@yahoo.com

ISBN: 9781095166994

Imprint: Independently published

Contents

"WHEN CONSTABULARY DUTY'S TO BE DONE,

TO BE DONE,

A POLICEMAN'S LOT IS NOT A HAPPY ONE"

So true. In the immortal words of Gilbert and Sullivan, a policeman's lot is not, a happy one.

Think about his job, what he actually *does;*

He, or she, is a "first responder" which means they are the first ones we call for

help when there's a problem, social, personal, or for general help. When we make a call for help, usually we're upset, want someone in a hurry - right now! and that's what generally happens, they're there within a short time to take over.

On two occasions, I was involved in a crisis and when the officers showed up an officer hugged me. It was just what I needed. I calmed down and felt everything was under control. Normally you wouldn't expect an adult, a grown woman to fall apart, but I did a great imitation of someone who totally lost her mental balance at that moment. A hug made me feel secure, everything will be ok - and it was.

Unfortunately, not all situations with officers are so positive. Things go wrong and officers are perceived as using "excessive"

1

force. These situations are investigated and resolved. And these are the ones that hit the news.

As a personal note, I have found that the press is not always fair nor trustworthy in what they report - selling papers is their business and, the news they report is not necessarily accurate.

Of course, we all make mistakes. Reporters don't necessarily report skewed or incorrect information deliberately; they focus on their goal - money. But their mistakes and zeal can have long-term damaging results.

This I know from personal experience.

It's disappointing.

THE POWER OF THE PRESS

Whenever an issue comes up in society, and I feel the world needs my opinion, I'll write a letter to the local newspaper - to the Editor. The press holds a huge amount of power in controlling people's minds and people's thinking. Resolutions and beliefs are easily influenced, and tainted, at times, by the press.

When I lived in Honolulu, there were two major newspapers (I forget the names) which seemed to have opposing political views. I thought this was healthy; everyone gets two sides to and issue - wonderful!

Wrong! We were getting one side to an issue, both editorials cleverly disguised as "opposition." I was confused. I thought we were supposed to have various prospectives to be well-informed citizens. I didn't realize at time "news" was another name for "good business." - *money.*

At this point in time, being that I am a Communications Instructor, I have learned the many covert ways to control an

2

issue so that it's generally assumed to be accurate information. Also I learned the many covert ways to present an idea that subverts the issue, twists it so that the understanding of an event is confused, muddled and distracts from the basic cause, the actual event.

The "news" you get is what will sell the paper the fastest.

Today there is unlimited "news," dissemination of *words,* but there's almost nowhere to send a letter to the Editor. The "inews" is limited to your friends. Facebook, Twitter, email, and junk mail are the current receptors and disseminators of information. And, unfortunately with this limited, skewed source of "facts" the truth may be obscured, twisted, a half-truth or garbled bits and pieces.

And, people believe it! They argue over it! They debate it!

At one program, years ago, Johnny Carson said there was going to be a serious toilet paper shortage. He thought he was joking! The next few days there was a run on toilet paper and the stores sold out.

Don't be one of those people in line for toilet paper. Stock up on newspapers - catalogs.

I tell my students, "If you hear on the news, that a tree has fallen over in front of your house, blocking traffic for miles in all directions, go outside, look for yourself. *If you see* a tree in the street in front of your house blocking traffic for miles, then you can believe the news. Otherwise, believe *nothing!*"

I have a friend from England who has lived in the U.S. for many years. She believes in the press. She says, "Carolyn, how can they lie? There are so many ways to know the truth - how can they possibly lie?"

You need to be trained to spot the many ways the press controls you. The press can be a glorious means of helping people and also an insidious tool to control you.

So, let it be understood that when it comes to the press reporting news of police activities, the information may - easily - be skewed, incorrect and tainted. The paper's first duty is to sell papers - not news.

STATISTICS

Not everything is like the weather, "there's nothing you can do about it."

Police brutality has a cause; it doesn't just happen; we can "do something about it." Like losing weight or stop smoking, stopping police brutality takes effort and a clear understanding of how this malady affects each citizen.

We usually get our information about police brutality from the news. We have already discussed the possibility and probability of the news being in error - let's say that reporting may have "mistakes," honest mistakes.

This information, mistakes, truth and situations are translated into mathematics which are then removed from "reality." This "reality" is called "data," and becomes Truth - numbers don't lie. If you turn information into cold, impassive numbers, then the conclusion must be correct.

Well, "correct" as far as popular opinion can interpret.

At school I attended a speech contest by students. One young man told of his passion to be an accountant for the IRS.

He said, "Numbers never lie. Five is always Five - you can trust Five."

4

Well, the *number 5* you can trust, but in what manner is the number 5 used? What did 5 do that is trustworthy? In what context is 5 trustworthy?

Do you know the old Bud Abbot and Lou Costello money routine where Abbot (the crafty one) was always cheating Costello (the dumb one) out of his share of their earnings?

Abbot had a bunch of dollar bills and he would count out money in Costello's hands: "One for you; one, two for me. One, two for you; one, two, three for me. One, two three for you; one, two, three, four for me... "? Costello ended up with a few dollars, and Abbot walked off with considerably more.

Now there's a five I would never trust!

Since social scientists rely heavily on statistics, let's talk about statistics - how reliable are they? And, let's begin with the understanding there are three types of lies:

Lies

Damn lies

Statistics

This handy rhetoric was observed by England's Prime Minister Benjamin Disraeli in the 1880's. The possible (probable) deception of data is not a recent disclosure.

Statistics, like the skewed news, are tentative - who's data is it? What's the agenda? What is their demographics? What specifically were the questions? Graphs report the amount of something: how big, how long, how much... etc. All using numbers. So with some accuracy we can know the "how much" of something.

But the bigger question, the "why" of something is not included in the data - the relationship between the data and the results are not explained. The "why" of some thing is the crux of the research; the "why" of something is what we can relate to and the thing we need to fix - adjust, understand.

At one time the Reader's Digest magazine had an article about divorce. Since the Digest is a very conservative publication, I wondered what it would say about divorce.

As I expected, RD said the number of divorces had declined. More people were getting married and staying married.

I laughed to myself, "Not in California, Florida nor many other states. A low divorce rate would only be in the Midwest where people get married in church and stay married!"

In the next issue the RD apologized saying all their data was taken in the Midwest, farm country.

Don't trust all data. Do your own research. (And God bless the midwest for setting good examples.)

BRUTALITY - ACCURATE DATA, OR, OPINION?

Let's look at data from the police "brutality" standpoint. Keep in mind the word, "brutality" is a concept - it's an opinion, an expressed emotion, *not* necessarily a fact. The interpretation of "brutality" rests on what point *you choose* to emphasize.

No way there is one definition of "brutality."

I Googled "Police Brutality" to see what stats for this phenomenon was available. I found a bonanza of mis-interpretation, rife with opinion and editorializing. I focussed on one article which I will not name as it was so badly written, my critique might provoke legal action.

The author is, perhaps, sincere about wanting police "brutality" to be monitored and stopped. But there is no direction given, no suggestions on *how to change it.*

Since I am a trained Instructor in rhetoric, communications, skewed data and editorializing, these "tricks" stand out like a red flag - let me amend that. These are not 'tricks," but merely a result of ignorance, lacking education.

Following are some observations, opinions and paraphrased comments of the author. And, no, I did not editorialize nor did I skew any this information. I am one of those people who deals in *facts* and numbers; data, under some circumstances, are not necessarily facts. I can give you data off the top of my head - in fact I have done that in class to show the students how easy it to lie to the public.

These are not direct quotes; they're paraphrases from the Google article. My response is in italics.

1. A fraction of 17,000 misconduct reports (of police) are reported. More reports are not conducted because the **police don't think it's important.** *The author holds the **opinion** that the police don't think the misconduct is important enough to report. Data does not include what people **think - opinion.***

Opinions have NO place in a report of data.

2. An officer may be cleared of misconduct even if someone dies. *"even if someone dies". Again the author is editorializing. We have NO information on WHY an officer is cleared. Maybe someone lied, misunderstood, or was under the influence of drugs. Maybe that person would have died of old age...? And, is this "someone" - related to the incident? Or Uncle Harry who died in WWI?*

3. The author suggests we ALL want officers to be appreciated. *In accurate research, words like: all, every, never, are not acceptable. In accurate research we believe there "may be" room for error. I doubt **everyone, "all,"** appreciates officers.*

4. In police-killings, only 1% of the officers are indicted, but in the case of a citizen killing someone, the rate of indictment is 90%.

Of these indictments, of these killings, what was the event? Were the civilians doing rescue work? Were they first responders? Or were they involved in 7-11 robberies, sidewalk hold-ups, bank heists...? What was the circumstances that civilians, at all, were indicted for killing? What about evidence the officer may have against the civilian? How did the citizen kill someone? Self defense...? There is likely NO relationship between why an officer kills someone and why a civilian kills someone.How stupid can you get - and get your data published!!!

5. In America, averages show that a police officer kills someone every 7 hours.*Under what circumstances?*

6. The author states over year 2015, police officers **killed** 1,307 people . In 2016, officers **killed** 1,152. In 2014 1,149 people were **killed** by police.

The author is inflammatory and outrageous in this wording. Under what circumstances did this happen?

7. 43% of police officers agree with: "Always following the rules is not compatible with the need to get their job done."*(OK, this makes sense in ALL walks of life - no rules cover ALL circumstances.)*

8. 93.7% of the victims of police brutality involving discharge of a weapon are men.*(Well if most officers are men, then most men will have weapons - this is really stupid)*

The author of the report goes on to list and editorialize incessantly about police misconduct. More incredibly stupid (my opinion!) "data" is that more Blacks are killed by police in Georgia than in Oklahoma!!

Uhmm...., would that be because there are MORE Blacks in Georgia than in Oklahoma? I imagine by that reckoning there are more Blacks killed in South Africa than in Switzerland...?

Of course the data omits the cause of the deaths of the population - *why* were they killed? Target practice?

While driving down serene, beautiful Highway 280 to San Francisco, I was listening to a program about whether or

9

not to increase the use of tasers in the San Francisco Police Department. One young woman, very upset, called in and said the deaths from tasers from police increased 300% from last year.

That really sounds scary, doesn't it? I pictured bodies lying all over Van Ness Ave. In further discussion, it seems there was 1 death last year, and 3 this year, all year.

The woman deliberately twisted the data to suit her purposes. This, in my opinion, negates anything further that woman will ever have to say.

When you have "esteemed" authors, researchers, spokespersons, reporting such skewed, biased - *stupid* - reporting, then that contributes to the public perception of police brutality. They will look for brutality, impute it where it may not exist and then exacerbate any future police/civilian interaction.

Yes, there is police brutality. Yes. Yes! Now, the question is...

WHY?

I have NEVER read any clear, unbiased reports as to WHY some officers are brutal. Perhaps data would show that some people, officers or not, are cruel; they're either born cruel or because of life circumstances have become cruel or bitter from personal experiences. And data may show that physical cruelty is usually male behavior. Females are cruel, yes, usually psychologically cruel at times, but male cruelty, in general, seems to be more physical.

And in general, public opinion seems to shut down when some women are cruel; it seems if the public doesn't experience the cruelty first hand, it didn't happen. Often women get a free pass for violence.

Perhaps, the officers, after working with the public in negative circumstances, day after day, minute after minute, the constant criticism, negative teasing, getting spit at, things thrown at them, the stress of having to live up to an impossible image of all things to all people, is a bit heavy.

And, above all, the bad press. I have long contended the press will say *anything* to make a sale. I have very little respect for the press, in general. I have been involved in circumstances where the press gave completely incorrect information and it wasn't challenged. Be careful what you believe in print or on the news.

Do you think that officers *choose* specific neighborhoods to go into, or perhaps they're called in or assigned there…? Do officers have a choice of what neighborhood to go into? Do the officers

11

make the neighborhood unsafe, or do the people living there make it unsafe?

What would happen if you dialed 911 and no one came?

And, some teachers are cruel. That is, perhaps, even more insidious than physical cruelty. Mental abuse lasts forever, it damages someone forever and very likely, cannot be healed. Physical injuries may heal easier, in a shorter length of time.

You see how I "generalized" the offense of cruelty...brutality? These words (among others): *Perhaps, may be, it seems, possibly, probably...* are all words used to modify an event. Probably nothing - *more likely than not* - is 100% good or bad in an event.

CURBING BRUTALITY - Ideas

Perhaps one way to curb brutality in any form, in any level of society is to have serious in-depth screening of the persons we choose for public service. People working at jobs such as: public interaction, teachers, police, doctors, nurses…? Librarians…?

Yes, it would be expensive, cumbersome and time-consuming to screen so many people. But, it might eliminate to some degree the source of public maltreatment. And, of course rotating the personnel in each specific area, would have each person learning each other's jobs and responsibilities, a better understanding and, perhaps give everyone a sense of renewal, of relief.

And, it might be beneficial for those who complain about police treatment, to understand and experience, the impact of their actions in a situation.

In one college I taught, the students were required to grade the Instructors and also the student was free to talk to the Dean or the Chair of the Department of any concerns. Sometimes just offering to listen helps a negative situation.

EXCESSIVE FORCE

Brutality is not acceptable, nor necessary - ever! However, "excessive force" may be necessary at certain times.

In society, today, there are drugs, powerful drugs that can warp a person's brain, turn someone into a "dead head" where he or she is out of control. Sometimes when a person is out of control, they have superhuman strength. It takes more than one man, really a MAN with a lot of physical strength, to slow down or restrain someone crazed on drugs.

People under the influence of drugs are out-of-their mind, quite literally.

Thus the use of tasers, sprays, cuffs and choke holds are needed to subdue someone "out of his mind". It might be beneficial to have someone who complains of "excessive force" try to contain a person out-of-his mind and then understand the need for "excessive" force.

Perhaps we need to rotate the police and the jailers - never mind the unions. If the police are going to be accused of brutality then all officers of any description should rotate jobs just to experience the problems and the craft of each other. Rotating jobs might ease the stress on the various duties so officers could expect to have a "breather" at times.

For awhile I worked for the United States Postal Service - the post office. There are basically two sets of jobs, clerks and carriers.

There was a great deal of friction between the two crafts as each side had no idea of the difficulties and problems of the other.

I was a Carrier (postman) for a brief period, then I switched over to clerk. So I easily understood the heavy responsibly of the Carrier and the difficulties of dealing with with the public and misaddressed mail. It's a tough, demanding job.

Then, as a clerk, it was was easier on the psyche. The clerks had to get the mail to the carriers and often the addresses were often scrambled, wrong zips, and also take care of stamp and product sales to customers - a nightmare!

14

Often Carriers and clerks got irritated with each other because we didn't understand the responsibilities of each other's work.

And I want to add, the supervisors were useless, rarely ever available to handle problems. Confidentially, your stamp money goes down a rabbit hole.

On an #endpoliceviolence site entitled "Addressing Law Enforcement Violence as a Public Health Issue", the 2018 Statement was concerned about racism and loss of control over community issues. Please note, these goals are totally non-factual, all "hope" and no "fact".

My interpretation of what I could glean is, that it's a wishful thinking of a group of well-meaning people who base their direction on what "should be," but devoid of reality. As Shakespeare would say, "A tempest in a teapot."

I will attempt to explain their "address" the best I can. Exactly what is "it" that they are addressing? I don't know. I couldn't locate the actual "address," but there were thank you's and acknowledgments of supporters. It seems this was a response to the Address itself.

Apparently the group holds the Public Health as an agent to use its influence and resources to "define public safety on their terms and to reclaim community control over public resources."

I have no idea what that means. The article goes on to say:

We believe it is Public Health's role to end racism and state-sanctioned and state-funded violence. May we continue to interrupt & dismantle stale and outdated racist ideology, speak up even when our voice shakes, reclaim our budgets, build relationships, build community-based strategies to addressing harm, divest from the carceral/policing system and build movements. Let's invest in thriving, vibrant, and healing communities! (There was no source given for the comment.)

End "racism," "state sanctioned and state-funded violence." How? *How* will Public Health end "racism?" Specifically *how* does the state "sanction violence?" Exactly *how* does the state "fund" violence?

This type of community action is energetic, well-intended, but utterly meaningless. It is rhetoric, obfuscated allusions to individual and community violations. Perhaps the organizers of the movement are well- meaning people, but who lack in-depth information on public funding and public issues, a complete ignorance of data, research and conclusions.

On the other hand, maybe I'm missing the point - maybe I don't understand the back-story. But how can I learn if the information is vague, double speck, lacking definition - **facts**... As the old saying goes, "There are three sides to every story - yours, mine and the Truth."

A cause, a movement has no meaning, no teeth, without facts. *Why* is there violence in the community? *Why* are the police called in? *Who* called the police? Someone in the community? *Why?*

What is the population of that community? Did the police just walk in there, clubs drawn, guns at full aim, mace elevated ready to burn the eyes of the community - and burn the eyes of the police? Mace floats around the area, you can't actually *aim it* at a target.

Or, did someone call for help? Did someone in the community put out a cry for help? A cry for help from the first responders? **WHY** were police called in?

16

How would the community feel if the police didn't show up? Is it possible they can settle their own disagreements? Or, would they be accused of taking the law in their own hands? Does the community feel it's "not their problem"? All too often, after the emergency is over, people stand around and mutter about "What they should'a done was..."

In some communities and in some opinions, it seems the police are damned if they do, and damed if they don't.

When I was a kid people used to say, "If you don't like what's going on, do it yourself." In other words, get in and get your hands dirty, don't just stand by and criticize someone else for trying. It's so easy to criticize some one else' efforts as a by-stander.

Give the police an alternative - specifically, what should they do? **Specifically**...

Not some blather about, "What ya should'a done..."

Amazingly and astoundingly, I have actually heard a citizen tell the police (on the news) what the police "should'a" done. At least twice I have heard this instruction:

A man, apparently out of control, waving a gun haphazardly around him, appears to be in the act of indiscriminately killing someone - anyone. His eyes are not focused, he is not focusing on anything, he is staring into space and the policeman, directly in front of him is saying, over and over, "Put the gun down! Put the gun down!" to no avail.

When someone is out of control, giving them instructions is utterly pointless. Eventually, having no alternative, facing a loaded weapon, the officer shoots and kills the offender.

Later it's discovered the "gun" is a toy and incapable of killing anyone.

It's at this point, the bystander, speaking from behind a parked car for safety states what the officer "should'a" done.

The officer should'a asked the gun-wielding, out-of-control person to "please put the gun down and let me help you."

Also it is noted that the out-of-control person is 16 years old! Killed! At 16!

Up goes the cry! **POLICE BRUTALITY!**

This is frustrating for everyone.

Recently on the news a woman was suing the police because her nose got broken and she was roughly handled in a protest for "rights". It seems in order to protest some political inconvenience, she was lying, with many others, on a major state highway, blocking thousands of commuters in the evening traffic rush hour.

The traffic was stopped for hours because someone was perceived as "not getting their rights". I believe it was when the American public voted for Donald Trump and not Hilary. Some people were outraged to think the result of the American process of election was not to their will - this time. Other times it was ok who we voted for. So, this time they had a tantrum and blocked the public highway.

The police were called upon to clear the thoroughfare, the major arteries of State traffic, and, since she was a component of the problem, she was forcibly removed.

In the course of being forcibly removed, she got her nose broken.

(Of course she could have simply obeyed the law - gotten her nose out of other peoples' rights by getting up and off the highway. That would have kept her nose intact.)

At what point do people's rights conflict? Whose side of the conflict do the police select to enforce? The thousands of vehicles on a major artery - buses, ambulances, tired taxpayers wanting to get home, mothers with screaming kids who need to go potty - the mother, too… doctors getting to the hospital…what about their rights?

All vehicles pay a tax to use that road - it's not free. Protesters are denying these motorists their right of passage, their right to happiness - get home to dinner and peace of mind.

The police are caught in the middle. They get aggravated, annoyed, dead tired, sick of this shit… They want to get home, too, and get their rights to pursue happiness.

Maybe the public should sue this woman for their costs in aggravation…?

POPULATION OF EXCESSIVE FORCE

Who are the police using "excessive force"on? A bank clerk? A bagger at a super market? A college educated citizen? A homemaker, factory worker? Good citizens, or, repeat offenders?

At one time I owned a small apartment house. One night, very late, one set of tenants were causing a disturbance. They were drunk and unruly.

I called the police who came out right away, grabbed the offenders, walked them over to the squad car and slammed them down, face first, on the hood.

I winced from the sound.

Interestingly, the offenders didn't blink an eye! They were used to it, and so were the officers. The officers were so used to drunks disturbing a neighborhood, their task was to quiet things down as soon as possible.

19

It was obvious to me the offenders took their treatment indifferently. And, really, if you or I were slammed down on the hood of a car, wouldn't you say, "I don't like to be treated like this. If I learn to act like a decent person, I don't have to be treated this way."?

I would promise never to be naughty again.

It is well within the grasp of an offender to change what he does if he doesn't like what treatment he gets.

Now about here, some Liberal will say, "Not necessarily...or, you don't understand." Maybe the Liberal doesn't understand.

By the way, I had a talk with the tenants the following morning about the disturbance. I told them, "That will not happen again in my house - do you understand? I will not have people behaving like that here."

It turn out the tenants didn't want these people in their home, and when I said "get rid of them, or else," it was the perfect excuse to stop them from coming over.

It never happened again.

Good citizens contribute to the welfare of the nation. They work and pay substantial taxes for municipal benefit. They have no time for graffiti, home invasions, robbery or assault. This population of tax-paying citizens has a right to a peaceful life. It's their right to go to work without fear, walk the sidewalks in peace, go home in the evening with the belief that they're safe. They understand the police are there to safeguard their right to the "pursuit of happiness."

But, not everyone understands the need for cooperation. Living in accord with the neighborhood and not disturbing the peace of their community should be a normal, appreciated mode of life.

However, as we say, "bad stuff happens." Someone, out of ignorance or malice may purposefully disturb the peace of the community and destroy the "right to happiness" of the community.

Some people in some communities seem to have a lot of nothing to do. In observing the daily activities of some populations, it seems they have no jobs, nothing to do that benefits the tax-paying, law abiding citizens or contributes to the infrastructure of their local society.

The young people are not in school, and those who are in school are not necessarily focused on learning. Some times the school is a refuge from the nightmare of home life, fear of going on the street - the potential physical harm from just being alive...

It is not unusual for young people - kids, to align themselves with the idle young restless people on the street. When you have nothing to do, you easily gravitate to crime or nothingness; it's like a hobby or a way to pass the time until you get put in jail. Why have ambition? For what? I have everything I need - weed, an iphone, whatever is the current brain-dead substance to stay away from responsibilities.

These people contribute nothing to society, but are leeches, takers, use-less.

At that point some people will step in and protest, "We have to understand them!", "They just need a chance..." HOW?

This cannot be tolerated - we do "understand" them. They have nothing they *choose to do* that is beneficial to the community. They *choose* to drop out of Life and then turn to crime to support their life-style.

If someone disturbs the peace of the community, even one person, this assault needs to be apprehended, stopped. This condition is the seed of police "brutality."

The "game" starts and gains momentum, the cycle of their life.

The problem is, *how* to stop it. The calm, logical minds of some people see a confrontation as a "misunderstanding" and should be approached calmly and with reason. This is absolutely the right thing to do.

It's like the "game" of cops and robbers we played as kids or cowboys and Indians, one side makes mischief and the other sets chase. Both sides have fun - adrenalin pumping, eyes, ears, alert. What fun!

But, when the same people repeat the same crimes for the same reasons - a distaste for education and work, then law abiding citizens need to depend on law enforcement assistance to ease the strain on the community.

Citizens have a right to the "pursuit to happiness."

In meeting the public call for assistance, often officers enter a very hostile atmosphere where criminals and also some of the community attack the officers - for sport. To control this attack, officers may have may to use "excessive force." Often people say, about the officers, "You should ask them first (the offender) before you save us - see if they will be nice." Well, maybe one of the community could ask…?

Let them try it.

Here's a suggestion:

Some drug-induced, repeat offender wielding a knife is coming at you, eyes wide open, seeing nothing, muscles bulging, and you just say something like,"Excuse me, but I think we have a misunderstanding. You need help. Let's talk about this."

No, you'll probably scream something like, "POLICE! POLICE! SOMEONE CALL 911!" You probably won't say, "Officer, I think we may have a misunderstanding here ..."

Then, when the police show up and take charge you have the Monday morning quarterbacks standing safely aside, saying "What ya shoulda done was..." And then send a letter of outrage - brutality!, to the press.

Once on my computer, someone sent me a film of a scene inside a jail. A young girl had just been brought in and had refused to hand over her belt when the jailer requested that she hand in all "dangerous" possessions. (You can hang yourself with a belt, shoelaces...etc.)

This young girl was no stranger to jail and chose to fight with the jailer over the belt.

The hand-shot film was apparently sent to me as a model of brutality. The jailer was trying to take the belt by force and the girl was strongly resisting.

My comment was, "Why doesn't she just give him the belt, follow the rules, and act like a decent person?"

The girl well knew the rules and chose to put up a fight. She well knew the risks involved when you resist an officer.

The film was taken off the site.

The purpose of the scene was to incite me to outrage over police "brutality." But, for me, the whole exercise was a monument of stupidity.

The problem of "brutality" rests with the citizens, the populace. There would be no "brutality" if bad behavior were stopped before it starts. Stopping brutality is in the power of the people.

We can make basic changes in bad behavior if we put our energy and *common sense* to work. It takes cooperation to stop brutality and perhaps reduce crime.

The public needs to get involved curbing brutality. However, people are basically selfish - if it doesn't affect "me", I'm not interested. Or, my favorite ploy people use to stall responsibility is, "Let's study the problem…" In other words, shelve it.

Well, this *does* affect *you*! - me, him, her, them… As the population continues to increase, as the density of the cities increases, the cost of housing and food increases, crime will increase and police brutality by default, will increase also. And taxes will increase. These are high stress conditions.

Is this who we are?

In general, uneducated beings who prey on others, weaker people who cannot help lift themselves out of darkness? When people need help to step out of darkness into Light, how do we help them? Give them a handout? Give them money? How does money, *specifically,* help people move from darkness into light? Money is a temporary bandaid on a gaping wound.

What to do? Where to start to seriously reduce the need or purpose of crime, hence the use of excessive force? In what ways do enlightened citizens help those who cannot help themselves?

THEY JUST NEED A CHANCE

There is a certain lovely woman, one who is the epitome of correctness in society. Let's call her "Grazialla. She is warm, loving, sharing and when a friend needs help, she's the first to show up and put her shoulder to the wheel.

In her pot luck dinners, she makes the best desserts.

Grazialla goes to church on Sunday, tithes, actually listens to the sermon and then goes out to lunch with friends, all single, older women.

She pays property taxes and conscientiously votes in all civic events, local and national. She's up on the issues and what the candidates' wives wear. An absolutely good citizen.

One of her major themes of change in the community is the prevalence of crime. In her community of pristine lawns, housekeepers, gardeners, clean BBQ pits and bunny-shaped bushes, quite often someone breaks into the camera-loaded yards, garage and rooms in the homes and takes jewels, family heirlooms, but, even worse, they take all the "iequipment"- all their means of communication has been callously aborted.

As of this moment, her home has not been ransacked. Being an older women, Grazialla has a dial phone, and a TV that still gets, "All in the Family" (no fornicating nudes or the "f" word) so there's not much problem of a break-in.

When a perpetrator (in an up-scale community, crooks are called "perpetrators.") is caught, apprehended, nabbed, her recurring theme is,"They just need a chance..." Thus assuming all crooks are helpless puppets of Fate.

Recently on the news some young man was apprehended and cited for burglary. He had a list of 28 previous convictions. Apparently he had devised a simple plan of life-style, but was not very good at it.

When hearing this news, I wondered what her definition of "chance" would be here? What sort of "chance" do you hand someone with 28+ convictions? How many "chances" does society hand you to help you become a good citizen?

When someone "needs a chance," what would be the logical thing to do…? Maybe give them a chance- literally. What sort of "chance" would you "give" them? More understanding, sympathy, increase in public benefits, mental health care, a lecture on diet, a drug rehab program… one, or all means of help?

Maybe send him to jail for R and R., counseling, hot showers, meals…?

Then, what if nothing helps? What do we do then for society to focus on this needy, lost person? Since the poor criminal is lost, maybe it's time for someone to *take charge?* - shove, drag, pull the poor, lost soul into a clearer direction of life?

Like, I mean, don't take excuses for *why* he or she is a lost, pathetic, loser…

Yes, they have rights - and so does society. We have a right to see that our taxes are spent wisely, not lost on people who choose not to advance themselves in their own life. Society has a right to expect positive results from those in need to do well.

Grazialla had nothing to do……..but, it was not like time was wasted. Most of the afternoons were spent with friends and she'd discuss how criminals just need a chance, over and over, how they just need a chance… she often served a cool mix drink or chilled white wine.

"IDLE HANDS ARE THE DEVIL'S WORKSHOP"

It seems I read this mantra on the Dead Sea Scrolls, which go back to…uhm…the time of the dead sea…maybe the B.C.'s?

Perhaps if we give these criminals something to do, their hands and brain will not be idle. Perhaps, training, a job, an apprenticeship, perhaps basic schooling?

I am a Yankee - no really, I am. I was born in Massachusetts where everyone has something to do. If you have nothing to do, you find something to do. Life is very simple there - find something to do and do it.

Apparently some unfortunate people who are victims of police brutality do not have "something to do." They get into a life of crime in order to keep busy. Therefore, those of us who are not victims of police brutality should share our life style with these unfortunates.

To help these poor, unfortunate lost people, we do have welfare, that is money handed out to poor people to help pay for food, shelter, weed and iphones. And the welfare money is mailed to their current place of residence to save them the inconvenience of physically going after it themselves.

This plan is to help lower the crime rate, hence decrease police brutality.

Someone came up with the theory, "If you give people enough money, they won't go into crime." After almost a century of ever-increasing welfare funds and ever-increasing crime rate, no one has noticed that the theory is invalid.

Something is wrong…

I just reviewed some Statistics about who's on welfare. Oh! The stats are SO garbled, all the data is explained in twisted terms concluding: The "welfare is mostly for the care of children."

How many children are we talking about? There's no answer to that.

Whenever you want to "con" someone, bilk them of money, time and "love," just mention "children". It's the magic word. If you don't buckle under the thought of poor, starving children, you are obviously made of stone - hard hearted.

Pathos, all pathos, prick your conscience, put you on a guilt trip - it works!

How many children are we talking about? There's no answer to that.

Maybe they haven't been counted yet. Maybe they can't count fast enough.

Then the obvious question comes, why are there so many children on welfare?

The reply was, "Well, they're not on it that long."

As we noted previously, "that long" is not a fact. It is an indeterminate amount of time - a useless response.

When no answers are apparent, we have to surmise, guess, theorize - curiosity will win; we'll create answers. Answers that people create can be very "loosey-goosey", in serious need of an audit - or education.

The common reasons "created" for women having a lot of children is:

    1. It's God's will. (We have free will - God's gift.)

    2. They want to.

    3. They have a right to.

    4. They don't know what causes pregnancy.

    5. They have an uncommon amount of male friends.

6. They have babies because it pays off, and pays very well.

If the public cannot get accurate answers, the public will create answers and that can lead to a social mess. We, the public, could very easily conclude that women on welfare have babies to stay on welfare - free money and so easy to get - takes so little effort and absolutely no education.

If you want either a good laugh, or a moment of rage, research the statistics on welfare payments to unmarried mothers. The numbers go all over the place and stop nowhere. It's like a Bernie Madoff accounting system where we taxpayers are the "investors" - somebody's making out BIG, but it ain't us!

Hawaii, Massachusetts, Connecticut, New Jersey, Rhode Island, New York, Vermont, New Hampshire, Maryland, and Washington, D.C., pay annual benefits worth more than $35,000 a year - I assume to one recipient. The median value of the welfare package across the 50 states is $28,500. There is no tax on welfare income.

You can get a lot of Mountain Dew with that.

It is my contention, my conclusion, my unshakeable belief that to reduce welfare is to reduce crime - they're two sides of the same coin - Siamese twins.

However, this is not to say that welfare is the cause of crime, police brutality. I am stating that these seems to be a strong link that welfare contributes to crime and brutality.

In the pretty little city of Mountain View, CA, was a woman and her fiancé who had 15 children and all of them were living in one room at a motel.

They were on the news, en masse, pleading for money. A rather young girl was with the group saying she had done all she could for them. She intimated she was cutting them loose.

So, in the quest for funds before the TV camera, the mother stood in front, her 15 children pretty much filled up the background while the mother begged for help.

The scene was almost comical - a Gilbert and Sullivan plot. People got themselves in a mess and wanted us to contribute to the mess.

Her tall, lanky boyfriend lounged on the bed in the background with his head on his hands. He had a moment of rest until his next opportunity to impregnate his friend. He looked very healthy.

Well, I guess you'd have to be healthy to impregnate someone to the tune of 15 children.

I wondered what impact that humiliation had on the children - how did this begging affect their self-perception?

WHY 15? Why any?

As for me, I would ask, "Why? Why does she have 15 children? I certainly know *how* she has 15 children, but, WHY does she have 15 children… ?

I can understand loving children, wanting a family - but 15? And she has no husband, no income, no education, no home, no stability - it seems there is a problem here. Something has gone very wrong.

Who is it responsible for that "wrong"? Who encouraged, sanctioned her to bring 15 children into this world - a woman so ill prepared to meet the daily challenges of feeding, clothing, cleaning, educating, civilizing, hugging, reading to…all those children?

Those of us who are mothers can mentally tally the relentless hours of: preparing breakfast, preparing lunch, preparing dinner, planning the meals, shopping daily for fresh fruit and vegetables Serving the meals, cleaning up the mess, doing the dishes. Empty the garbage... *it never ends...*

Just doing the meals is a full day's work. Then you have the laundry, folding clothes, towels, etc. Get them off to school - on time! Have them do their homework when they get home. Have a snack ready for after school.

What about after-school sports? Do the children have any quality time with the single parent? Piano lessons? Community service?

What kind of quality life, personal attention, personal affection, can 15 children get from one parent - even from two parents?!

And, in particular, from a woman who has no education, no skills, no way to support *herself* much less 15 additional souls!

Insupportable!

So, who allowed her to slip into this morass of despair, ignorance, and poverty? Who encouraged her to have so many children so thoughtlessly? The "do-gooders" rely heavily on her rights to have children - especially people who refer to the Bible as sanctioning, as encouraging, this travesty.

Who is it who puts these 15 children at risk for a life of despair, of ridicule, of hopelessness into a cycle of possible crime, drugs and possibly an early death?

You did.

I did.

WE are responsible for her life's conditions, and, by default, 15 additional innocent lives she brought into this cold world. Additional lives who are doomed to a future of disgrace, poverty, humiliation and ignorance.

And, very possibly, a bleak future in prison, on the streets, or, dead from crime related acts, selling drugs, hold-ups…

I have actually heard University students say things like, "She has a right to have as many children as she wants!"

And, yes, she does. But then, I say, she should pay for them - why me?

In the interests of care, substantial, healthy, positive care for those 15 children they should *immediately* be put in foster care, or in an orphanage. It is obvious the woman, and her fiancee, have no means to care for the children, and, it would seem no ability nor interest in attending to their personal and positive growth needs.

And sadly, you and I really believe additional funds will correct this problem. You and I really believe we're doing the right thing, the Christian thing. When I bring up the inequity of handing out money - rather than education, to the "disadvantaged" I get labeled "selfish," cold-hearted, that I don't understand, followed by looks of disdain.

Then, after pointless discussions, after a guitar sing-off about how, "Yes, they'll know we are Christians by our love, by our love, yes, they'll know we are Christians by our love…"

About then all the Christians smile benevolently, hug each other with Christian warmth, leave, get in their SUV's, go home and dust their 4 bdrm/3bth home to get ready for the cocktail hour. The governess has the day off, but not the kitchen help. They're tired after stumping all day for the "poor" - let Jose start the BBQ.

I can't help but wonder, if I bought 15 Mercedes and couldn't pay for them - insurance, motor maintenance, garage, oil job... would you jump in to pick up the payments? Would you understand (I'm POOR for God's sake!) I can't help my longing for 15 magnificent machines that I have no license for, nor know how to drive - no place to park?

I doubt it. You would probably snort at the preposterousness of the idea and say something like, "Are you crazy! You bought 'em - you pay for 'em!"

And then I, as a University educated Liberal would say to you, "You just don't understand - YOU are selfish!!"

But, I really feel, underneath the clamor, that somebody's making out big time in the welfare game. The "free" money is loosey-goosey in many ways...? So do we really want to stop this cash cow, do we really care about the people? Or, do we want to protect the system? I have no facts, just a feeling.

Welfare reform is pointless as long as we, the well-meaning, noblesse oblige, the University educated, continue to advance on a treadmill... wearing our ear plugs to listen to music...

WORK AVAILABLE

The overwhelming majority of people on welfare have two arms, two legs, a reasonably well-functioning brain and voices that demand their rights! Their definition of "rights" is skewed; they have more than rights - their treatment from society is far above the average working person who relies on his wages and nothing more.

Is there some reason why people so well endowed physically cannot work?

What?

You say there are no jobs?! I see "jobs" everywhere I go; the streets need sweeping, broken windows need repair, plugged toilets at the park need attention, pull weeds in vacant lots, comb beaches, clean creeks, remove trash from empty lots - and needles! Oh, there's lotsa needles everywhere, in the park, beach, under trees, in vacant lots, oh, yes, lotsa needles.

They could clean gutters, clean graffiti - all this to do (Yankee philosophy) plus go to all the "Help Wanted" stores and fill in applications.

This is the tip of the work-available iceberg, as I see it.

The likelihood of having a job would probably not give someone enough time to get into mischief, break the law, use crime and pathos as a means of income.

I understand there are women's jails where they do have job training. They teach esthetics, hair styling, make up and nails. At least it's something. I would also have dental hygiene, computer science, accounting, data processing, pre law...and this would be along with reading comprehension, composition, spelling, basic math...some basic, useful stuff.

Of course this program would include on-going counseling, helping someone to choose a better life style, individual and group counseling.

And, some social skills would come in handy, yes indeedy, very handy...

WHAT TO DO ABOUT OUT-OF-CONTROL WELFARE BREEDING?

I'm going to propose a reasonable solution to excessive breeding by young women. Girls should not be encumbered with such grievous responsibilities in their youth. This is the time to grow in self respect, develop inner strength, find out who they are, develop their talents, skills, make life-long good friends. This is the one and only time girls have to grow up.

There is an old German saying:

Too soon old, too late smart.

My suggested solution is in several parts:

1. In low-income neighborhoods (or, any neighborhoods!) for girls you have meetings to explain welfare procedure - an orientation.

These classes would include clear instructions on birth control:

A condom has a 63% accuracy in preventing pregnancy. that means there is a 37% chance a girl will get pregnant.

With a pill there is a 38% chance to avoid pregnancy. That means there's 62% chance of getting pregnant!

With an implant, an IUD, an inter-uterine device, there's a 2% chance of getting pregnant. That means there's 98% chance of maintaining control over a girl's life to pursue a her education or a career. To join Life with normal people and hold her head up high!

There is no, good, excuse for an unplanned pregnancy.

2. If she gets pregnant and has no means to support the child she has choices she can make.

3. One choice is to give the child up for adoption.

4. Another choice is to keep the child. If she makes this choice it's up to her to prove she can provide adequate care for the child.

5. If she keeps the child, the father must pay for half of the support. The county will assume the other half.

6. If the father will not pay for half of the support, then the child may be given up for adoption, or be put in foster care or an orphanage.

7. If the mother insists on keeping the child and expects the public to support it, she has an option.

She'll be enrolled in school where she will attend full time, get satisfactory grades and her goal must be toward a skill or vocation.

The education will be paid for by the community. The mother will have room and board at a specified location and some stipend allowed.

Since "I'm" paying the bill, she will not have her own apartment, the living arrangements will be in a controlled, safe room, probably something like the YWCA, in and out guests monitored.

While she's in school, her child will be in an approved child-care facility. This way the mother can keep her child and work toward her education and self respect.

8. If she has a second child under conditions that she cannot care for the child, the child will be put in foster care or up for adoption. Obviously, if she can't care for the first child, she can't care, at all, for a second.

9. The mother will be expected to attend and learn basic ways to avoid an unplanned pregnancy. All babies have a right to be wanted and cared for.

10. Drug testing will be often and sporadic. No un-prescribed drugs are tolerated. If the mother is on drugs, she'll be put in a facility to get cured. The baby will be in foster care.

Babies-for-profit, for income, will not be tolerated.

If the girls are unmarried, unattached, this solution applies. If they have a husband, or live-in male friend, they get nothing and maybe lose the child. The welfare of the child is paramount. If two attached people have a child or children, they have no access to public aid.

Often the sperm donor is incarcerated (as they say on the "judge shows"); it's the nice way to say the fathers are in jail for an unspecified amount of time.

The community would need to have a hotel with room and bath, cafeteria, laundry and a door-keeper at the entrance for their security. The young mother would be provided with an education, care for her child and drug-free security, all on the community.

This would be infinitely less expensive than caring, perpetually, for multiple births in less than adequate conditions - motels. Especially it would profit in terms of self respect.

37

The community would have the satisfaction of knowing the child is raised in a cared for, healthy environment. The children would be raised by people who are educated and who would model dignity and self respect. Their world would be a safe place where there is no need for violence, home invasion or drugs. They'd never experience "police brutality" nor parental abuse.

I just read a saying on a cell phone:

Forget about abortions, they're not important. Treat abortions the same way you treat foster children - forget about them.

Painfully true. So often in my classes my students are almost 100% against abortion. They say things like:

The girls can get help, there are organizations to help them.

Then I ask my students who are single mothers, "Who was there to help you through you pregnancy?"

Without exception, they all replied, "No one - only my mother."

My conclusion is that the Right to Life people and the Pro Life people are, for the most part, phonies. They don't put their money where their mouth is. They're careful not to get their hands dirty with facts, with Truth.

My observation and interaction with Pro Life and Right to Life women is that they are rigid, self-satisfied, cold women, punishment-oriented. I wonder what Freud would say about them?

BIRTH CONTROL

It's unfortunate the term birth "control" is the accepted wording for the creation - or not - of a new life. Perhaps the concept of a "choice of whether-or-not to make a time-consuming, money consuming, life-time responsibility" would be more accurate.

To an American the concept of "control" is abhorrent. We prefer to think of ourselves as **"free!"**, we can make **free** choices! This is a **free** country - have as many kids as you want! You have rights! If you have a child, you *choose* to have it.

Well, it's not "free," and you should not have "as many kids as you want" - unless you can provide for them. As I have said, "Why should *I* pay for *your* children? No one paid for mine - I did!"

On a judge program one woman being sued was a 24 year old single woman with 7 children. The judge asked why she had so many children and no income nor husband. She replied, "Accidents happen."

Are 7 children an "accident?" Maybe she should find out why she is so clumsy.

The judge asked her why she didn't get a job. She replied that she would as soon as she got on her feet.

My thoughts were, "Well, if you get off your back, you can get on your feet."

Another girl, age 20, single, had 6 children she admitted to in court!

Who sanctioned this child having 6 children before she had grown up herself?

Who, in their right mind could see this indifference, this ignorance, as a way to raise children? Is this breeding "reasonable" from any perspective? What about the children's rights? What about their "Right to Happiness"?

For society - *you and I*, to allow girls, uneducated girls, the privilege to have children when these girls are not nearly mature, not legally responsible for their actions, not financially nor emotionally stable yet, no emotional nor financial backing, and above all have no concept of the grievous responsibility of motherhood, is tantamount to abuse -

Child abuse!

Yes! Child abuse. When I read of the customs of other societies, religions, how female children are married off to older men, some girls are sold, like cattle for slaughter by men, girls are impregnated by males - raped! I am incensed!

And yet, it happens here, legally, every day in front of our noses and we sanction it, you and I, sanction this child abuse. We call this abuse "well fare"!

We don't overtly sanction this child abuse; it's that the people can't help themselves - they need money, they need help, they're not educated - blah, blah…

Is this a society "under God"?

Do you and I see this travesty? The travesty you and I sanction?

This junket is where somebody intelligent should step in and take "control." We should point out to people that you just can't continually breed without heavy responsibility to the child and to society.

Tonight on the news was another incident of "police brutality." A fourteen year old "skinny" boy was wielding a gun in a public area. The police were called in to handle the problem.

One officer showed up and ordered the boy to put down the gun. The boy refused. The officer ordered the boy several times to put down the gun, but the boy kept swinging the weapon around his head.

The officer attempted to subdue him and the kid punched the officer in the face. The officer then called for help. Eventually four officers could not restrain him, so an officer shot the boy and killed him.

This entire scene was filmed by some by-stander.

Later, at the station, the mother was in a rage that "her kid would ever do that, all a lie, police brutality, a mother knows her kid, you get a feeling..." incessant raving.

Very likely the mother will sue for police brutality, using up tax-payers'

money and police time. Nobody wins. And, will we ever know how this boy got the gun, what was wrong with him.

Will we ever know "why" this happened, and "why" similar future incidents will happen - as they surely will?

BOYS, YOUNG MEN

So far I have focused on the problems of, the misperceptions of girls. I have focused on the incidence of pregnancy to single, young girls.

But girls don't get pregnant alone, it takes a partner, another agent to impregnate them - boys.

Boys, in general, have a peculiar position in life - in almost all cultures. The expectations border on the unreal. They are expected to be "man"ly - "take it on the chin", succeed in sports, academia, be tender, strong, decision-makers, calm, repairmen of all things...it never ends.

The pressures on males to succeed, in all countries, is unreasonable - insane.

The boys, young men, under the stigma of welfare have these ludicrous expectations enlarged, magnified, beyond reason imposed upon them.

The probabilities are: They're born to an unmarried girl, there is no father in the home, there are numerous male models revolving around the girl, but no stable male models, no warm, caring models - just males - who quickly come and go.

So how do they find identity? How do they find the comfort of male strength and bonding?

THE GANG AS SURROGATE FAMILY

It is human nature to bond, to form groups, socialize, identify with people of your own kind, "birds of a feather...". Humans need the warmth, approval and company of other humans. We are a societal creation.

If there is no warmth and approval in our present society, a human will go, seek out, or create a society of his own - a group, or gang to identify with. The gang becomes a surrogate family.

And, because they perceive themselves as "men," they behaved in a way that is imputed to males, having a son. How do they have "sons"? By impregnating girls, "manning" it over girls, controlling girls to prove their "man" hood.

The girls misinterpret this attention as "love," no one loves them at home, they'll find "love" as they can, where and when.

> On another "judge" show, a single, girl explained why she had babies. "My boyfriend said all his friends had a kid. He had no kid, so I gave him a kid."

"Gave" him a kid. This was to prove his value, his manhood, and her love for him.

So sad.

The cycle continues. Children born to single mothers, children bereft of a warm, loving family will turn to where they can find love, on the streets, in jail.

Jail is secure, predictable, organized, meals on time, showers, health care, some entertainment, a family… why leave? Why not make every effort to stay there?

And when a group of illiterate, uneducated, intelligent, energetic boys form a group, anything can happen. Studies have shown that most people are followers, so, if you're in a gang you will, more likely than not, do what the gang does.

Obey the rules, conform, "group think," become invincible, the status of gods. I recently followed the actions of a gang who believed they were invincible to bullets.

They weren't.

In a circuitous way, these gangs are created and supported by society. We provide them with an excuse to break the law. Not only do we provide them with material comfort, in jail, but by doing so, we add to their status, their importance, their value as "men." The badder they are, the more of a man they are.

CONFLICTING DATA

It seems anytime there is a subject of any controversy or conflicting opinions, the data will reflect exactly that. The data I found concerning crime and welfare as to who, how much and as far as related to crime, information on that was very sparse and muddled.

So, it seems that for some reason data, accurate, unbiased information on welfare, multiple births and the crime rate as far as a cause-effect, is highly guarded information from public scrutiny - well, is either highly guarded, or ignored - or not recognized as a cause-effect.

Or, here I go again with my penchant for suspecting ulterior motives in money handling, I strongly feel much of the straight-forward data of how, where and to whom the money goes, is deliberately scrambled under the code of "departments," "being studied," "reform," ad nauseam. Money evaporates...

If you track police brutality backward where there are crimes by children, you will find poverty, shame, and a desperate cry for love.

If you track young criminals backward, you'll find a cry for recognition, nurturing, family identity.

And if you track backward the relationship between the criminal and his "nurturing," you will likely find welfare - poverty.

There is no nurturing. No individualism.

Try as they might, Liberals, Socialists, Communists, - any inclusive "ist," will *never* be able to crush a person's spirit. A human's core is *individualism*. *Each* person needs to be recognized, nurtured and accepted.

Yes, we are social beings, but also we need self-appreciation, recognition for a job well-done. Self pride. Respect.

That's why it is imperative to understand children are not "cheaper by the dozen." Each child is unique. You can't have it both ways.

The "do-gooders" believe they're doing just that when they encourage, or, at least condone that the individual spirit be warped to fit the needs of "other."

On one side of their mouth they say, "We're all alike."

On the other side of their mouth they say, "Well, that's the way he is - you have to accept him like that! Well, what if HE doesn't want to? You have to allow for differences!"

Liberals say, "You can't say that! You can't do that! We each have our rights - you can't tell people what to do - you have to respect their rights. " ????? HUH? "Liberal?"

Their psyche is hopelessly screwed up. Their way of life has everyone miserable.

And, if you peer into the cause of poverty, you will likely find multiple births in a single parent home.

Why single parent? Perhaps because of lack of alternatives, no education, no job, no choices but fleeting relationships. Perhaps each relationship brought with it the hope that this would be a lasting relationship, someone to love and care for and

have that person care for you.

Everyone deserves love, warmth, caring, with a special person. A special person you can depend on, who you understand and that person understands you.

The fact that most relationships, at that structure of society, have the same learning experiences, similar upbringing: no nurturing, no models of how to behave, no self respect demonstrated, no security in the home, no organization in the home...

At times I have heard interviews with young girls - 12, 13, 14 years old. They were asked, "Why did you get pregnant?"

The sad answer was, "I wanted something to love. Something of my own."

Going backward, then, we can assume the girl had nothing to love, no one to love and no one loved her. In her world she was alone, alone at such a young, tender age when a girl is most vulnerable. She had no one to talk to, no one to hold her in esteem - care about her, only her; she had nothing...

If this the life we want for America's children?

Think of boys under the same circumstances. They can't reproduce; they can't have a baby to fulfill their longing for "someone to love," "someone to love them."

They are truly alone, they have NO ONE - no body to hold them close, assure them they are a good person. And to do that, it takes a MAN. A woman, a mother, can do something, certainly offer love and support, but a boy needs a MAN.

Life in a revolving door brings men "in and out, around and around," but not a father, the one person who looks like you, holds you up as special - "my son..."

How that "aloneness" must hurt. How, day after day of being unloved, unwanted, a meal ticket, must wear on his little psyche. There is one way out, one way close by, easy to get, the life of crime. An acceptance into a fraternity of brothers who need each other, understand each other and "love" each other.

And, the bigger and more daring the crime, the more respect, "love," a boy gets from his "brothers."

Thus, the need for police brutality. It's not "love" the boys experience,, it's a cry for attention, a cry for Love.

Life is a cycle, a treadmill, not forward, not backward, only the appearance of making headway - delusion.

Welfare is a delusion of gain, of respect, of a positive identity.

46

This frustration in itself would cause a lashing out, a frantic reach for change, improvement, respect, only to realize the "lashing out" is grasping an illusion.

How frustrating. These dead-end of life choices would possibly end in "getting even" with society - the "haves."

Which, again, leads to crime.

> *My neighborhood is populated by professionals who worked hard to get where they are, years of school, years of training, internships, trial and error. They finally reached a point where they are financially comfortable.*

> *On Halloween, a bus, sponsored by a non-profit brings bus loads of under-privileged children in our neighborhood to see our homes.*

> *After these trick or treaters leave, the flowers in our gardens are trampled and the houses egged.*

> *If we complain, we're called "snobs." These children are disadvantaged, so seeing our homes vandalized is seen as "understandable."*

> *Is this sick?*

If the "do-gooders" in society really want to lift people up, it starts with the child, his quality of life. "Quality" cannot be provided by numbers; it has to be select, supported and tracked - and sincere.

But, as I have mentioned, does society really want reform? Or do we covertly want to be "better" than someone else? Does society need someone down so we can be up; we can be superior?

For every problem there is a solution; do we seriously want a solution to police brutality, crime, lost children and lost souls?

Or, is "understanding" them sufficient?

PREVIOUS ATTEMPTS AT WELFARE REFORM

Of course there have been previous attempts at welfare reform. None of the studies about welfare reform linked welfare to crime and police brutality that I could find.

But there is a direct link as far as the statistics go. I'm going to assume the failure to link crime to the image of welfare is because associating crime to benevolence is distasteful to society. Generally most of society chooses to believe that people on welfare are needy and grateful for our help.

And, I'm assuming that this is accurate - people on welfare do need help. the question is, "who is really in need of help, and who can help themself?"

The following research I refer to is provided by the Health and Human Services. The data was all over the place; one report says "...welfare is out of control." Other data says, "...recipients are happy, system working well." More data says, "...system intolerably confused, conflicted, not enough funds to really help, too much government paperwork, forms complicated..."

The data was all over the place. There was nothing reliable as far as data goes. You could find any data to support any conclusion you advocated. Totally useless.

BUREAUS OF BUREAUCRACY

Somewhere I read there are 84 government agencies to help needy people. That is one agency 84 times, redundancy, a deluge of forms, each iota of information required is based on another form at a date which has expired, for the applicant.

The duplication of words, but each word having a distinctly different meaning than those in the other forms - a different language, is overwhelming, crushing, to the applicant.

Ironically, the applicants are understood to be semi literate, reading comprehension minimal, perhaps a non-extant grasp of mainstream American English...this is almost laughable!

I am well-conversant, comfortable, flexible in English, American or British, and I am at a loss to fill out these forms - most forms! The reason being usually the people who create the forms have no idea what they are asking.

The questions are obfuscated, tangled, duplicated...oh, need I say more?

And, there are 84 forms of them. Is this a great country or what?

Eighty four forms.

Here's an adventure I feel compelled to share. A times in my life as a divorced, working mother of two children I was forced to seek government help to survive. As I mentioned, filling out the forms was a nightmare and I needed help. There were two women at the Social Security office assigned to handle my case. And, I noticed we were not of the same race.

The two ladies were very rude to me and turned me down. My situation was so serious, to me, I wrote to my Senator, Dianne Feinstein, and complained. In short order, I was reinstated to the same two ladies, who were very annoyed and let me know it.

Another time, another lady, not of my race, either, but a different racial origin, was very kind to me and helped me greatly. Also, to my delight she told me of secret words that get immediate attention to anyone who accepts the forms from you.

So, in my trying to get assistance, I learned two things: Some administrators are racist. And there are secret words specific to use for immediate help. There are certain code words that go in certain places in certain forms that the clerk immediately recognizes you as your being "one of them".

I cannot give you the code words as they are specifically for that form - so sorry. But, what I learned is that not only are the forms themselves a hideous obstacle to assistance, but the administrators may be prejudiced either against you or for you.

Good God, what a nightmare for people who are not well-educated and can't stand up for themselves!

TANF

Temporary Assistance for Needy Families is a government organization requiring people to get a job within 2 years. The problem here is, few needy people have sellable skills. They need school, they need **BASIC** education, on so many levels.

"Basic" here is not a suggestion, it's imperative.

Under this organization a family is covered for 5 years or less depending on the state. If they have additional children after signing up, they may lose all benefits. "Assistance" translates to money, cash or checks.

Also, the hidden cheese in this labyrinth is that there are few jobs available to someone who has no or little education and no sellable skills, It's a catch 22.

ACA -

Affordable Care Act

Also known as Obama Care - almost incomprehensible to the above average college graduate. If you are not Phi Beta Kappa - give up! You'll have a heart attack trying to figure it out.

If your household income is between one and four times the poverty level, you can get insurance credits on your health premiums. ...sort of...

Good luck.

CHIP

Children's Health Insurance Program

President Bill Clinton designed this medical coverage program for children under 19 years old when their parents make too much money to qualify for Medicaid but can't afford private insurance.

SNAP

Supplemental Nutrition Assistance System

Formerly referred to as "food stamps," this nutritional system is devised to encourage you to use the assistance to buy nutritional foods.

A great idea, but do people who eat pizza all the time, know what is "nutritious"?

The people on the street I see eating are scarfing down fast foods as fast as they can. Perhaps SNAP should be monitored for fruit and vegetables, only. But that puts a burden on the stores.

SSS

Supplemental Security System

Interesting. I could find nothing on Google under this title. Perhaps, somewhere in the misty cottonwood trees of Missouri is a government office staffed with eager assistants, waiting at the phones for someone to call in and request an incomprehensible government form for the Supplemental Security System.

Maybe no one told them they don't exist…? Their paychecks are stacking up in a warehouse…?

So sad.

CNS

Child Nutrition System

This "system" is totally incomprehensible. I imagine those who are "assistants" for access to this system will be staffed in OZ or a corn field in Kansas. The Wizard is at the door-slot waiting.

To get into the system there are two steps:

    1. Obtain an NICD., and

    2. Request access to the School Nutrition Technology Program.

That's it.

HUD

Housing and Urban Development

Funds to help qualified people pay for their housing is paid to the *agencies* that manage the housing for low income residents. This helps the residents pay for housing - rentals, that they otherwise could not afford.

So the residents do not get the actual money, the money goes to the agent who rents or manages the property. Every little bit helps the resident here.

SECTION 8 (Housing Act)

Housing Assistance Section 8

This is rental-housing assistance paid to the landlord, the home owner, to help low income families pay their house rent. This Section is administered under HUD.

Also under HUD is the Housing Choice Voucher Fund , which can be applied to rent, or the *purchase of the house of your choice.*

I wish I had known I could get a house for "free" - stupid me! I paid for my private home out of my *wages*. What about you?

Is this a great country or what!

MEDICAID

Both the State and Federal governments join hands to combine funds for health care for low income families, children, pregnant women, the elderly and disabled.

Another note of caution from personal experience. I had private health insurance for years, then I needed to sign up for Medicaid. In order to qualify for Medicaid at that time of my life, I had to pay an $18,000.00 fine!!

Being a simple minded person about "Federal systems, aid, programs...etc.", I pleasantly asked the nice lady at the SS window, "Why am I being fined for something I never used?"

She said, "Excuse me." and went into another room. I never saw her again. After sitting in the hard chair for some time, I left.

If anyone out there in Federalala land can explain that math to me, I'm all ears.

JOBS

A Basic Skills Training program (JOBS) of 1988 was a law to encourage the tendency of Americans to acquire training for jobs. it reinforces the Americans work ethics. They want jobs, not a hand-out. The law does not provide any location nor method to get training for work. But - it's a law. We can always use another law.

PRWORA

Another law enacted by President Bill Clinton in 1996 was to "end welfare as we know it." Evidently work brings happiness and fulfillment." But finding a good job is a challenge when you need money on an on-going basis, and need it now.

This funding is not just a paycheck, but a sense of fulfillment to help people get off welfare; it's a component of self-worth and happiness.

Apparently this law was not too well known, Possibly because people really didn't want to work, or because they couldn't recall the acronym.

Myths About Welfare Programs in General

It seems there are myths, fables and rumors about how welfare people think about their civic duties.

In general it is believed that:

Welfare people don't vote. They are too busy surviving to go to the polls. They have no interest in the issues.

People on welfare are mostly Democrats, the "free money" party.

Immigrants come to America illegally to have their babies and stay here by public sympathy to become Americans.

Then this data shows that Illegals cost Americans far less than American citizens. The numbers are:

Babies born to undocumented mothers cost 15.5% of Medicaid, while American-born welfare mothers get a whopping 16.1% of their bill paid by Medicaid.

Undocumented immigrants only get 1% of the welfare payments.

Native Americans get 1% of the welfare aid also.

Undocumented immigrants get only 9% of the cost of food stamps.

Whereas only 16% of the cost of food stamps is for Americans.

My question is, why are undocumented immigrants getting *anything?* What does an American get if we're in *their* country?

is this ok…??????

PRWORA

Another law enacted by President Bill Clinton in 1996 to "end welfare as we know it." Evidently work brings happiness and fulfillment." But finding a good job is a challenge when you need money on an on-going basis.

This funding is not just a paycheck, but a sense of fulfillment to help people get off welfare; it's a component of self-worth and happiness.

Apparently this law was not too well known, Possibly because people really didn't want to work, or because they couldn't recall the acronym.

THE RASMUSSEN REPORT

On this report I am hopelessly confused. So confused I can't even be sarcastic.

"A 2018 Rasmussen Report survey found that 61 percent of Americans believe that too many people are dependent on government financial aid." (Google)

The report goes on to denounce this belief as being without a clear understanding of the tax usage. It suggests that the people who think too many people are dependent on aid, do not know that their states receive the most aid by the way of federal tax cuts, federal grants and contracts.

The report goes on the conclude:

"Those states get aid in the form of federal aid, this is supposedly a tax relief, But if the welfare population, specifically, were reduced, the residents would get less federal aid which would cut down on their taxes." (Google)

Well, whatever this reports contends, it certainly can't be denied! Or supported! Or agreed with! It's a meaningless manuscript of a Dali painting.

I wonder if Rasmussen went on to become a stand-up comic…

For instance, "just as George W. Bush's compassionate conservatism proffered a series of special tax incentives to prop up religious institutions, reformicons want targeted tax breaks to strengthen middle-class families. Some want to restrict immigration and trade, just like unions of yore."

In nine states — Hawaii, Massachusetts, Connecticut, New Jersey, Rhode Island, New York, Vermont, New Hampshire, and Maryland — as well as Washington, D.C., annual benefits were worth more than $35,000 a year. The median value of the welfare package across the 50 states is $28,500. no tax on any welfare income

RASMUSSEN IN SIMPLE ENGLISH

I asked a Master in Economics to explain, simplify or justify the Rasmussen Report and (I think) she offered a clear explanation.

Imagine taxes as being in two parts, 1. Free money for the over-population of welfare recipients, and, 2. The dire need to support infrastructure for the well-being of the populace as a whole - such as: hospitals, schools, sidewalks, police protection, street lights, sewage, fire department, library, jail, prisons, sports, bridges, dams, water treatment, sewage treatment, dumps, coster care, handicapped amenities, highways, traffic control

Even as I write this the money appropriated for the benefit of the entire population as compared to the overwhelming cost of welfare is clearly unacceptable. The populations who contributes nothing to the state health gets an overwhelming amount of money to continue to contribute nothing - except more population to support.

The Masters in Econ explained that even if the taxes were reduced for welfare, the amount of money from taxpayers would not decrease because the infrastructure is so depleted the same amount of money would be needed to attempt to catch up with past-due expenses.

In other words, all taxes would be used to try to catch up with the projects now in arrears, so taxes could not be reduced.

Well, all the more reason to try to catch up with the *needs of the populace* as opposed to handing out blank checks to imbalanced, money-gorging welfare recipients?

It might be cheaper to give a bonus to each welfare recipient to not get pregnant...?

The system of welfare in inane, vacuous and out-of-date. You should NOT get something for nothing!

Does anyone care?

FILLING OUT FORMS = HIGHWAY TO HELL

When I was first in college I decided I was smart enough to file my own income tax - what could be so hard?

Full of confidence, I sat at the big kitchen table, spread out the IRS form. Name, address, SS number. The fourth line down said, "Put the sum from the amount on page 14 here, sign and send it in."

? I was on page 1, line 4. What sum? Page 14?

They were serious. I thought for a moment it was a tease to make us laugh and then get down to business.

No, they were *serious* - I was livid!

As a college student, I was stymied. Think of what people of less education go through when they fill out government forms.

Forms are in a code of initials and numbers which are privy to the employees, but hell for the applicant. Forms are a labyrinth of numbers, "go back to page 97, pick up the sum on Line 18, transfer that sum to the Family Residency Situation, Section B and add the Proof of Need section under C.

Then go to page 11F, Section 12H under Income from bi-lateral indulgences as reported in Term limits (page 7D)......

Seriously, does anyone really think these forms are fill-out-able by people who are hungry, out of work, saddled with expenses and a crying child in a full diaper - and maybe some grave illness looming over their head? Think of the incredible stress!

It's ludicrous!

This idiocy of forms is pervasive. Forms for school, medical care, loans, I.D., credit cards - anything you need requires a form. I have often thought that if some organization were sincere and intelligent, before offering their forms to the general public, they would have a panel of 15 people chosen at random off the street, invited into the inner sanctum and asked to fill out the form.

If 14 of the sample group had an easy time with the form, it was successful. But if all 15 broke down, slung chairs and water bottles at the walls - there's a problem.

For people in need, the disadvantaged, people who are confused, hungry and desperate, a form is the last thing they need.

Yes, we must have information, but perhaps they should give out the forms piecemeal, over a period of time. Give people in need a chance to think, pull themselves together and then help them with information better gauged to their understanding.

SHOVELING SAND AGAINST THE TIDE

No welfare "reform" program mentions the prolific increase in births of unmarried girls. The reform programs do not touch on one possible cause of police brutality being based on underage welfare dependents.

If the girls continue to reproduce, welfare assistance is like shoveling sand against the tide - we'll never catch up. The girls *must* be taught to respect themselves, to respect their dignity, have self pride. There is no respect in producing a quantity of children; it is the quality of a child that is desirable.

Only a child who is planned for, wanted and loved can be blessed with the concept of "quality". One mother cannot adequately have time for herself, the rest of the family and give one of the family attention needed for a state of "quality".

Girls should be advised that in order to have respect from society and in their personal lives they should hold themselves to higher standards than indiscriminate pregnancies. You cannot respect yourself if you're available to use either for added income or to impress others.

One young lady, on welfare by her admission referred to herself a a "diva." She said if a man wanted to date her he'd better bring furs and diamonds along to give her.

How sad for some young, pretty girl to believe that respect and "love" are locked in "things" and not in one's heart.

WHAT ARE WE TEACHING PEOPLE?

If the enigma ended there, that of those who contribute nothing get far more in material gain than the tax payers, the problem of police brutality would not be as egregious as it is, maybe even disappear.

But, when people get something for nothing, it's never enough. Like King Midas, they want more and more; they want everything they touch to be the best and the most without costing them anything. They don't understand that the true cost is their self respect.

To achieve their goals - something for nothing, these "disadvantaged", turn to more and more violent means. When police intervene to protect the working people, the police get spit on, rocks, bottles and other objects thrown at them and they are vilified. It would be an easy assumption to understand even the most well-trained officers would get angry and, at some point, react violently to save themselves.

As Martin Luther King stated, "violence begets violence."

Since the working class cannot stand up under such unreasonable expectations, cannot provide the welfare recipients that which they have come to expect, some welfare recipients take a short-cut to increase income – crime; some welfare recipients get out of control and find crime pays well.

By now they have completely lost any sense of self respect. They have translated the acquisition of "things" into self-importance. Jail time is a tattoo of courage on their arm. Jail is a fraternity. Their values, once fragile, have been usurped by the collection of "things" that show daring and heroism in their level of society.

They may riot; break store windows of working people - local merchants, grab cell phones, expensive handbags, etc. - they'll get what they want one way or the other, because, they have the shield of being "disadvantaged," a "poor thing."

Who's going to come down on a "poor" person for trying to bring himself to the level of the more fortunate citizens? It's all pathos from here on out.

Statistics on the relationship between crime and welfare recipients is readily available. The stats show that many welfare recipients spend their welfare money as soon as they get it and then turn to crime to supplement their income 'til their next check arrives. Evidently welfare recipients feel they are entitled to procure what income they need in what manner they can.

It's worked so far!

And, the really sad thing is that they prey on each other. If their lives weren't bad enough, they have fear of their neighbor, scared of their neighbor - "What's he going to do to us?" is a common theme.

How does all this relate to police brutality?

Police are not psychiatrists, not psychologists, not social workers, not counselors, not baby-sitters; they are law enforcers; they maintain law and order. For some people, this is an inconvenience – law and order is for you, not me, seems to be their credo.

We are teaching people they have a "right" to get what they want. And, because they are "disadvantaged," they have the "right" to get what they want anyway they can get it - we'll just have to "understand."

"You need to understand them," is a common refrain among the "do-gooders".

How "understanding them" stops crime is a link the "do-gooders" consistently overlook. "Words," "condensation," "tolerance," simpering smiles and a tipped head are not adequate.

But, it does stall taking any real, getting your hands dirty, reform required.

SELF PERCEPTION - ENTITLEMENT

Herein lies the problem, those people who assume they should have what they want and not work for it. They assume their "rights" should be met at any cost, take what they want when they want it. They are entitled because they are "disadvantaged."

In some cases the same people who are repeat offenders get off with a hand-slap; they're released as almost as soon as they're taken into custody. Then, the chase starts all over again. Deja vu. What a waste of taxpayer money and court time.

The officer has been endangered for nothing, very frustrating! It is understandable why those who are assigned to protect law-abiding citizens become bitter, angry and aggressive. Instead of backing up the people who protect us, many ignorant people condemn law enforcement for not taking the time to "understand" the criminals - be patient and courteous under intense stress. You try it!

There is an old ferry that transports tourists around Alcatraz to Angel Island on San Francisco Bay, The ferry is old and not "handicap ready."

A broad, high, flight of stairs connects the lower deck to the upper deck and there's no railing to steady yourself on the stairs when the ferry rocks.

That day a number of "disadvantaged" children were running wild on the deck, having a wonderful time playing chase and ducking in and out of the crowd.

I was on the stairs, concerned about falling, when a boy of about 8 years shoved me aside to run upstairs.

I yelled, "Hey! Cut that out!"

Immediately, a young, serious college- age girl walked up to me and ordered me to apologize to the boy! I was stunned! She explained the boy was disadvantaged and they were on a trip for him to have fun.

This was his first lesson in entitlement.

I was so shocked, I actually apologized!!

Later I reflected on what that young, innocent, dim-witted college girl actually taught the boy. She taught him to disrespect other people. She taught him that his needs came first, ignore the needs of society. She taught him that he can use any means he chooses to get what he wants. She taught him to achieve his needs, his wants any way he wants, he can turn to violence, because he's disadvantaged.

Now, tell me...do you think this child has any incentive to change? If his social "superiors" sanction violence, what course do you think he will choose in his life?

Then, assuming he does turn to violence and crime, can you imagine his confusion when he gets picked up, roughed up, by the police? He was doing what he was taught to do, encouraged to do, and encouraged by the same people who send his check every month to help him improve his life, and shove old people around!

In my field of Communication it is apparent there is serious lack of familiarity with non verbal communication and rhetoric. The "girl" was obviously out of her depth - she had no clue what she was doing. She meant well but that ain't good enough. She needed some maturity and life experience before she'd be able to realistically assess her inane perception of the child's behavior.

On the other hand, the young man was sharp - he picked up the vacuous perception of the girl and ran with it! He really was a bright kid!

This cycle must change. Crime is not cost-effective. If we substitute education in place of welfare in an attempt to reduce crime, everyone benefits.

This pattern of crime gnaws away at even the most stalwart of police officers. It is understandable that they release their frustration by physical expression – unnecessary excessive force. How do I propose, logistically, we do this?

Perhaps one way to discourage entitlement is to make the punishment more severe. Evidently "understanding" the criminal, "nice," is not getting through to the offender. Make jail a really unpleasant place to go and I don't mean by abuse, I mean by insisting on an education. Learn a skill or stay in jail until you do!

Instead of being sentenced to a measurement of time, maybe people should, also, be sentenced to a measurement of achievement. They maybe should be sentenced to learning short-order cooking, car repair, HVAC repair, architecture, tree surgery, telephone lineman, plumber, astronomy...

And if their crime is really egregious, sentence the offender to learn Russian, Chinese, English, calligraphy, Mah Jong, marriage counseling... And they can't pass the class, or get released, until they are proficient.

By the way, these classes should not necessarily be within the offender's range of knowledge or choice. The point of education is to *grow, get outside of your comfort zone.* If we don't know a person's abilities, run some test-tries before them and see what his/her abilities are. Don't assume that "he can't do that!"! Find out!

Seriously, make jail unpleasant and personally profitable!

Education is a tool, it's a weapon against the vicissitudes of life; it's mental balance on a churning ship of fools.

As long as there is a "captive" audience, put the time to good use. Make offenders learn Latin irregular verbs! Seriously - that will deter crime! This especially works well if someone is in solitary confinement!

Yes, I joke but I'm serious. Lack of socially acceptable skills is a handicap to anyone who wants to turn his or her life around. Teach social skills. I forced my adult college students to put their hand over their mouth when they coughed or yawned, They were not allowed to chew gum or have any "toys" in the classroom. I'm a teacher, not a playmate.

I had two male students drop my class because they resented my telling them to put their hand over their mouth when they yawned or coughed! I guess they showed me!

PSYCHOLOGICAL DAMAGE

When you were a kid in school and everyone lined up to be chosen for the sports' teams did your blood run cold at the thought of being chosen last?

In welfare *you are the kid that gets called on last...* Boy, that really hurts. It's a humiliation you never forget. Who wants you? You have nothing anyone wants - you're a loser. Yooooo are a loooser!

This is how it must feel to be on welfare. By doling out money, favors, guidance to people, who are basically intelligent - the disadvantaged, we are sending the message, "You're not good enough. I'm so much better off than you!Look at you, you've got nothing.

You can't do anything unless I help you - I'm better than you are.

In one school where I subbed for the 5th grade, one teacher would not allow the welfare kids to get the free milk. Most of the teachers were overtly hateful and the school was an unpleasant place to be. I actually loved the kids, but it was apparent they were very uninspired by life in general. So sad.

The kids came to understand from their "betters" - anything you have, I gave you! Anything you want, you have to ask me for it! You have nothing without me! (Imagine a cold, prolonged laugh here.)

What an insult!

To be kind, and talk down to welfare people, is even worse. Welfare people must get the message that we, their superiors, hold them in very low esteem. We, superiors, are amused at their antics to look respectful.

Look at the disadvantaged, and then look at us! Who are the winners here?

The children must grow up feeling like failures; they understand they'll never make it no matter how hard they try. They are shot down before they get up.

So, when it comes to crime, breaking the law, why not? What can hurt them? They're already at the bottom of the society heap. They might as well knock over a 7-11, bring along a big bag and a small gun.

You'd be surprised how many inches a small gun adds to your height.

Welfare recipients see themselves as losers even before the game begins.

As it stands today, the Life path of children on welfare is: Out from the womb…into the streets…into jail…into the streets…into jail… And, then, we pay for the jail, too.

In one of my Communication classes a young man was escorted in by a zealous, athletic young lady.

She introduced him to me and seemed to have some kind of message I wasn't picking up.

She explained, "This young man is from Georgia, recruited for the football team."

He sat in the back row and was very quiet. I assumed he was absorbing the material and did not yet have the textbook.

In subsequent days, it was apparent not much academia was going on in his life.He said he couldn't study because he had no textbook. I then realized he couldn't read. He had no clue what was going on in my class.

I gave him my textbook and told him, "Any time you need help, any help at all, even in your other classes - I'm great at everything except math - I'll help you."

His young lady escort asked me, "How is he doing?"

"Not good," I replied.

She gave me a stern look. "If he doesn't pass this class, they'll send him back to Georgia."

Well, I don't care if they send him to Georgia, where his family is! I will not be threatened to pass someone just so the team can win. I couldn't care less about the team! I'm an academic.

But, what really touched my heart was when he came running up to me on campus, "Miss Franklin! Did you really mean it when you said you'd help me with my classes...?!" His eyes were wide with amazement - someone cared!

Surprised to see him, I said, "Yes." He left and then I never saw him again. Frankly my heart broke. What will happen to him? Is he lost in the labyrinth of bureaucracy, the multitude of empty souls who look to the "Boss" for a handout?

Is he destined to end up in some police stranglehold? A young man - a boy, actually, so full of life, promise and hope - will he end up as a statistic on some indifferent list of lost souls?

69

How I wish I could take him home and put him- smack dab! - in the middle of my big, Italian family. He would fit right in!

The college where I taught seemed to care about the less fortunate population and to that end there were students admitted who were woefully unprepared for college. They had very limited verbal skills, no reading comprehension, no concept of how to study, what to study…

I guess the college assumed that by inserting these unprepared students into mainstream college classes, that the students would absorb knowledge by osmosis. I mentioned this improbability in a meeting of the Elite, and I got dirty looks for my trouble. Their assumption seemed to be, "You just don't get it!" - and worse…

And, incidentally, these bleeding heart liberals, PhD.'s, are the same ones who never return the emails or phone calls of frantic, confused students. These are the same Liberals who don't show up for appointments with their students. I've often thought, "Some day I'll walk by a professor's office and a student's skeleton will be hanging from his doorknob, waiting for Dr. Betterthanyouare to show up for an appointment.

Sadly, the students dropped out, one by one, scared stiff and completely discouraged. It broke my heart.

We need to have a school with grades between high school and college - as sort of "catch-up" school. We could give it some banal, uplifting name like, College Interim Prep" - fairly innocuous.

THE REAL "DISADVANTAGED"

I shudder to think of the outrage of bleeding heart liberals who feel making the "disadvantaged" go to work, have a job, is mean and unfair. The liberals believe that if you're "disadvantaged," you're not able to work.

How these two concepts are linked has never been clarified. Liberals keep their heads in a dark, warm place safe from logic. For starters, I'd ask, "How does one get 'dis-advantaged'?" The answer is obvious; people *choose* no education, no jobs no desire for improvement – they're comfortable!

School is FREE! - in America. If you don't go, you *choose not to*. Yes, there are impediments, bullies, slow-student development, terrible teachers, hard stuff to learn... But, it's free and gets you out of the rabbit hole.

Persevere!

Let's digress for a moment and talk about people who are *really* at a disadvantage in America. As a college instructor, many of my students are people who have escaped from terror, murderers, starvation and torture in their own countries.

Some of my students are boat people who have fled from their country at great risk, heading for America and freedom. And, many of my students are "illegals" from south of the border desperate for a better life free from crime and terror.

The first thing they do is get a job – they *choose* to work. It may be the lowest paying job available; but they provide for their families. Many of them *choose* school to lift themselves out of fear and poverty for a better life. If those people, who have no money, no jobs and don't speak the language, come to this country and succeed, why can't welfare recipients emulate these "disadvantaged" people and also walk with pride?

I have had "illegals" in my classroom. Technically, I suppose I should have turned them in. But, what better place for anyone to seek sanctuary than in a classroom? As far as I am concerned, a classroom is a holy place, untouchable by opinion of someone being "good," "bad," "right," "wrong."

Education is a place for a healthy society, intelligent, thinking people to guide us all into acceptance and understanding.

WE NEED ANOTHER CAESAR CHAVEZ

If you are not familiar with the dedication, the unselfish devotion to mankind of this man, Caesar Chavez, you absolutely should be. He dedicated his life to lift a whole people out of servitude into a world of self-respect. His life was a gift to the world.

In the 40's, in a time of deep depression for many Americans, the Mexican field workers in the California farms were badly treated. They started work at dawn, worked until dusk, no breaks, no bathrooms in the field and were often cheated out of some of their pay by the foremen.

After all, these people didn't speak English, had no education, worked at the lowest jobs - who cares!

The fat strawberries were wonderful!

California was heavily dependent on these people to pick the crops and get them out to market - big money was waiting for the land owners at delivery.

Not only were these people cheated out of their, minuscule, pay but the use of pesticides became very popular. The public had no idea how lethal these sprayed poisons were.

Farm workers were dying from inhaled gases and developed cancer at a high rate.

No one cared.

Except Caesar.

His selfless devotion, his love, education, know-how lifted this entire people into the Light. He stopped the excess use of pesticides, brought awareness to the *world* of how to treat humans with dignity.

His mantra was.

A MAN MUST HAVE DIGNITY

Caesar taught that no matter your lack of education, your lack of money, material goods - under whatever is your lifestyle, you have a right - a duty, to be respected.

When these uneducated Mexicans, not citizens, living in abject poverty, hand-to-mouth, no health care, no rights to protect them, had this man, this person who was one of them, step in the front of their abusers - physical abuse - physical, emotional and economically abused and Chavez challenge them, to win over them and prevail in the mainstream society, then they understood their value!

They had a right to respect! Caesar chanted over and over,

"A man must have dignity"!

Welfare recipients also need a champion, a strong leader who understands the need for education, uplifting, self-respect in the lesser appreciated segment of society.

"Free" money comes at a great cost to their self esteem, their self-respect and the loss of their talents is a loss to us all.

They need someone to teach them that having children is a serious, joyful, occasion that requires intense care, education and maturity in order to have healthy, well-adjusted children for a healthy society.

Quantity is not necessarily quality.

The welfare recipients need to understand that crime is not the way to self-respect. You cannot achieve respect by violence, that will result in the pointless lives of fools who end up going nowhere - a dead end life - perhaps, literally.

Self respect was a goal of Malcom X, but he based his actions on hatred, racism. Caesar was motivated by love, a deep spiritual love that is fed by belief in the good of men. Love will prevail - always.

Perhaps there is champion for the welfare population who will lift them up into the beautiful world of self-reliance and then they can have the joy of giving to others instead of taking from a benevolent, better-than-you donor.

If you have dignity, self-respect, you will not step down to violence, brutality, jail, pity - the negativity of Life. Violence only hurts the person who sinks to that level to exist. Those of us who know this have a duty to lift those confused people into the Light.

ANOTHER SOLUTION TO WELFARE

My solution? Put the majority of welfare recipients under the age of 65 to work. Since we're paying them anyway, money will be paid as wages, not as a hand-out.

Jobs can easily be created. Of course we know some will not show up on the job, be unsatisfactory employees - it doesn't matter - no work, no pay.

To do otherwise is discrimination; to pay people for not working, doing nothing, *is discrimination*, favoritism. Since the former welfare recipients will be receiving pay checks twice a month, they will have less incentive to commit crimes for added income. They will have two checks to look forward to instead of one!

The same government workers who send out the welfare checks, could keep their jobs. But instead of handing out free money, they would send out pay checks. The payees would pay income tax, just like people who are not "disadvantaged" do.

Welfare recipients would no longer be regarded as "lower" class citizens, "under privileged," "disadvantaged;" they could hold their head up with pride.

But, having said all this, we need to look at welfare from another view point – that of an insult, *which it actually is*.

SYMPATHY

Welfare is a covert message telling the recipient, "Here, you poor thing; let *me* give you some money. **I** am so much better than you.

You have nothing, are nothing, can do nothing unless **I** give it to you. Without *me*, you can't exist; **I** control your life, your destiny."

"Charity"…this is noblesse oblige – humiliating.

CHRISTIAN OUTREACH

For 18 years my Outreach assignment at church was to give a sermon every third Sunday of the month at Elmwood Jail in Milpitas, CA. It's a women's prison whose population is mostly young women with little education and raised, for the most part, on welfare stipends.

To increase their income they turned to crime, usually prostitution, selling drugs, and, all this with the "encouragement" of their boy friends. They had little self-esteem. That style of life was the only life they knew; they had no known alternative.

Being that I'm an educator, I wrote letters and attempted to make appointments with prison administrators to allow me to hold classes, free, to give these young women tools to meet life after prison, get jobs – keep them out of the cycle of crime and incidence of police rough-handling, "brutality."

The police have no incentive to treat these people gently; there is no cause to respect these people, they have no respect for themselves, so why should the police care?

The police see the same faces year in and year out - the stories, the excuses, the constant problems of these lost souls are boring, tedious and completely without merit. Who cares? Just get the inmates bundled in and out of jail, in and out of jail, in and out… It never ends.

And then the public expects the police to be "nice" and considerate of people who appear to have no value, no value even to themselves.

The persons in control of the prison system were not interested in the long-term ramification of getting off welfare, out of the prison system and easing the load on the over-stressed police. They did not respond to my request to teach for free.

I was very disappointed - what a waste of young life! And, as a Yankee - a waste of time! I saw "something to do," but was not allowed to do it! So unAmerican!

When someone works, he increases his value and self-esteem in the eyes of society and himself - respect works for everyone. As Cesar Chavez said, "A man must have dignity." Respect is a two-way street.

Education, independence and life choices give you dignity.

(As an aside, I am an Episcopalian. My services were very low key. I appealed to the girl's common sense and intelligence about changing their life-style. The girls are very intelligent, no one but me cared before about their intelligence. My message of education, choice, get-up-off-your-seat and make better choices, was a message they'd never heard before. It was a lecture the way I do in class.)

The services offered by fundamentalists was one of "God loves you," and 15 minutes of guitar and hymns. More "Jesus loves you!" - guitar, hymns and threats of Hell, "if you don't change." No guidance, no facing reality. Oh, well…

One time one of the girls asked me what do we feel about the "Evil One." I told her when you think of someone, focus on someone, you send that being energy, life force. I said we focus on God, the Life Force of Creation, not destruction.

She seemed surprised.

HOW SINCERE ARE WE?

Let's go back to the start of this book. If we remove the reason for "brutality" we can reduce or eliminate the brutality altogether.

Welfare sends a covert message of a person being "stupid," "useless," "poor," which, in itself may induce rage, a feeling of helplessness, being trapped in a dead-end life.

Do we *really* care?

With jobs and education comes pride, independence, an understanding of one's value to himself and his peers. Like the woman with 15 children, she had no job, no useful skills, no self respect - how does this affect the children's psyche, their sense of security?

At least in her case ALL the children had one father, her "fiancé." How can we Americans hold our heads high knowing there are children living in squalor - and we can do something about it?

CHRISTIANS

There are two kinds of Christians,

    1. Those who are intelligent

and,

    2. Those who play the guitar.

(on occasion, they overlap)

To me, Christians are inexcusably to blame for our social problems - seriously!

When there is a social problem, we need to solve it; of this we are inherently capable. Our trouble is, each denomination sees the problem a different way, when, *clearly,* there is one way to see social problems.

You look at *what* is happening, and then you find out *why* it's happening.

Daily, hourly, there are programs on TV revolving around murder, callous treatment of one another, degradation of women, rancorous home life, badly behaving children, selfishness…shall I go on?

Who watches these shows? Christians.

Screaming song lyrics, half-dressed "stars" command the TV, radio, iPhones and every possible means of communication. The noise deadens the sounds of nature, the sound of human needs.

Youngsters are impressed with the mantra, "If it feels good, do it." "Everyone gets high, what's your problem?" Ad nauseam.

There are people on welfare, people in prison, the homeless, teen suicide... why?

Because we have lost our sense of value. We do not respect ourself nor anyone else. We have no direction in life. Some years back, on two occasions, in church, I stood up at announcement time and mentioned the violence on TV. I said it was unacceptable and we should have a letter-writing campaign to sponsors to take the violence off TV.

The congregation laughed at me! One especially influential woman, pointed at me, laughed and said, "There she goes again!"

I noticed that none of the youngsters said, please, thank you, excuse me... how sad! It's a lack of respect and nobody notices.

Previously I had mentioned to the congregation that Christmas was to celebrate the birth of Christ. Most of the Christmas cards were deer, ducks, snow scenes, Santa, happy children - where was Jesus? As Christians we should send out cards about the birth of Jesus.

After church, one of the major members told me, "You have no business telling people what kind of cards to send!"

I was dumbfounded! Where did I go wrong?

Yes, we did play guitar at my church, and, yes, a great many members were intelligent. I was seriously confused - still am.

It seemed to me, many of the Christians felt if they tithed, that took care of their social obligations, the poor, the homeless, the abused children, battered wives...

Their concern for distressed lives was fleeting and shallow.

Our example from the New Testament of helping people, is to go where they are and lift up the lost souls. If people are "lost," they would have no idea what to do with money, a stipend, a drop of water in a desert.

We need to teach them the way to a better life, not pity them, not *hand them* what they ask for - let them work for it. Teach them a skill, teach them to think, explain that how knowledge, a skill, depending on their own gifts, is the basis of happiness and success.

As I said earlier, the Life path of children on welfare is: Out from the womb...into the streets...into jail...into the streets...into jail... - until the *dead end.*

A hand-out, pity, "understanding" isn't going to give them the good life, a life of self-pride and self respect.

If we really respect people and want to help them, get them off welfare and into schools. Stop poverty at the core. Stop girls from having babies they have no concept nor examples of how to raise.

Get them on birth control. Pregnancy is not a right!

And teach respect for authority. A little respect goes a long way.

MY PIANO TEACHER, MRS. HUBNER

My piano teacher, Mrs Hubner, was from the old school. You did everything right and you didn't stop doing it until it was right. She didn't do my practicing, I did my practicing. I did everything on the piano myself and practiced daily.

The only thing that confused me in learning the major scales was her "jamming" words together on occasion. For years after my lessons, I still wondered what "jibidee" was. In my old age, it suddenly came to me, "G, B, D" - "jibidee!"

A major, major chord!

When I told her I practiced on my Aunt Margarite's piano, an old, forlorn upright, where the keys "clunked", ivories missing, pedal hanging on the floor and if it ever had pitch on the strings, they were long gone.

My Aunt advised me, "It's good enough to practice on."

Mrs. Hubner became very annoyed, "Good enough to practice on!" She snorted! "It's at the beginning of learning when you should have the very best! You should have the best teachers, the best instrument and the best selection of music! How can you learn properly if you don't begin training with the very best!"

That comment made a deep impression on me. It's true! When you start out on a task, start with the best tools, the best teachers, the best equipment.

When starting with anyone on welfare, before the money is tossed out - the degrading hand-outs, focus on getting the people in school. Start with the sounds of the letters, the sounds of the syllables, the sounds of the words. Then meaning of the words and then the meaning in the sentence - communication!

Teach someone the foundations from the ground up and learn from the best. First they have a good night's sleep, a good breakfast, and come to school looking forward to the best life has to offer...

SELF RESPECT

For your further education of welfare, self respect and people in dire need of help, I strongly suggest you watch this film:

https://www.youtube.com/watch?v=3dh0Z0kLoKc

The film features Charles Murray, political scientist who advocates talking less about money and more about satisfying lives. (I cried all through it).

ABOUT THE AUTHOR

Carolyn Franklin

M. A. Communication Studies

M. A. Education

B. A. Psychology

30 years voice training (San Francisco Opera)

Voice/Speech improvement Coach

voicedynamicscf@yahoo.com

OTHER BOOKS BY CAROLYN FRANKLIN

Police Brutality: A solution

Adam: First man, or, first mouse?

Emotional Intelligence: Like yourself

Coping With Bullies: A gentle approach

You Can Catch More Flies With Honey: The Art Of Rhetoric, Persuasion, Manipulation, and Blarney

Your Voice – Your Personality The Total You

Women Bullying Women: An effect of Women's Lib

Rx For Your Communication Ills - The ULTIMATE Book on Communication

Women At Work: Win-Win Communication Strategies

#MeToo, NOW, Women's Lib, Just Say No: Why they won't work

Athena: Goddess of Communication Strategies

Welfare + Diversity: Social Suicide

The Story of Mary: Mayhem, mirth and miracles

How To Talk To A Texan And Other Foreigners: Understanding Everyone - We're Not All The Same!

The Princess And The Pee: Caring For A "Special Needs" Person

Just Be Your Self - Whoever That Is